Unless you know red…

Carol Argyris

For my family, with love and gratitude to them.
They make my life shine.

Contents:

Words

Are We There Yet?

It begins.

Geraniums

Scarlet geraniums licking at her feet,
a smile walks through flames.

Around her head
yellow leaves,
shifted by winds,
scratch and scrabble
at the margins of belief.

Her fragmented mind
falls in splintered crystals
to ground zero of the nether worlds
where it is reconstructed
as castles in the air.

Paradigms

The world is stirred.
Cosmic winds have turned against us,
disturbed our bubbles, burst them,
spraying us with soapy liquid,
blurring our vision momentarily,
shifting our paradigms utterly.
Our view is muddled.
Comprehension suspended
We are segmented, fragmented.
A Picasso. A Mïro.
A Chagall,
in which people float aimlessly through rooftops.

Lockdown.

I'm going to write a poem
About a hang nail.
About a sore bone.
About fat feet.
About hunger in the wee small hours
And how choc ices call.

Images rushing through the brain
are not unhinged or disconnected nonsense.
They make the puddingstone.
The conglomerate. They all add up
somewhere in this moment
of craze and cracking.
This apocalyptic cataclysm.

As the four horsemen gather themselves for duty
and Brunhilda, girding her loins, goes forth
to spy out warriors for the Halls of Waiting,
and the Good Lord hires nine cleaners
to reopen his thousand-roomed mansion,
his Air B&B.

This is the stuff we are made of at the last.
Billions of particles we try to name
move in orderly procession
around the fuzzy ball we call our planet.
The dust bunny in space.
Which could also look uncommonly like
coronavirus.

It's been a difficult week.

The skies have cried coldness on us,
battered, blustered us with fury,
rained on our parade,
frozen locks on cars, denied escape.

In the night fat hailstones
smashed spitefully onto roof tiles
hard as bottle glass,
blackening petals of fragile flowers.

Solar light warmed the air at midday.
Thought to cheer us.
But the blue it shone from
was watery as a psychopath's eye.

Eclipse.

Blanched of colour
the land falls into unnatural night.
Trees fade to tissue-paper cut-outs,
shadow play.
We watch the servile moon
devour her master.
Disruption of the established order
omen of times to come,
abandonment.
Bang on pots and drums.
Immerse yourself in water.
Pray

In bad moments

I pull in air
Find it unsatisfactory.
Empty.
Eat sharp cheese
Which turns to chaff
Worse
To bitterness
Through which the world is viewed.

Out there people walk on moorland grass
Sit on stone bridges
Warmed by sunlight
Dangle their feet
In icy water
Till toes turn blue
Whist I lie here on Memory Foam.

Once I ran my fingers
Through the oily wool of sheep,
Smelled the rot in pools
Where stagnant water trapped, grew green,
And rats slid into it,

Bad things were caught there
Things that needed antibiotics
To shift them.

My family:

I want you to walk through this strange world
in a cochineal cloud of love
Armoured in silken gold for your protection,
Shot through with green
for inspiration and clear thinking.
I want small birds with fierce beaks to be your outriders
To frighten away the dark.
To keep the fear at bay.

Spider.

She came to me on filaments of silver
Toyed with the straw of my hat
on some mission of her own
that I will never understand.
How she swung six feet above the paving
to reach from tree to table
I will never see,
but I am closer to her in this instant
than to any living being on Earth.

Normally
I would not have noticed her.

Rekindling.

Put a match to the fire
We are a brave species.

As darkness falls,
pulled by seven sorrows
too deep for tears,
We light the sky.

With suns of our own making
We warm our hearths.

Fear, perturbation, and thoughts on death.
inevitably rise in this unknown land.

Zombie Movie

The world is a zombie movie now.
No time to write before the hoards are on us,
stumbling, stinking, flapping their foul rags.
Enticing us to join them.

The unbelievable is indisputable.
Parts played by people who do not have Equity cards.
Every soul distinct and sharp. Miraculous.
Important. Irreplaceable.
What we had yesterday
is lost for ever.
Precious in its dying moments.

Poppet

I have created myself from air.
From thoughts that fly around me daily
 a shape has formed.
The threads that spin into my mind
momentarily, fraying into nothingness,
I've snatched at
given them importance
made them the poppet
to be dressed in hair and clothing,
bewitched, endowed with life,
of a sort.

What if these threads were all that was left?
The thin armour
I have conjured.
What if?
Would I be content to half exist,
mirrored in glass on the underground train,
as insubstantial as my fellow travellers are to me?
And will this poppet steal my soul
for reasons of its own
making substance of itself
whilst leaving me the husk?

Unless you know red.

Unless you know 'Red'
the word means nothing to you.
Unless you know the scent of a ripe peach
I cannot share it with you.
Unless you know grief I cannot tell you of it.

Unless you have tasted the wind from the sea
I cannot convey to you its salt-weed tang.
Unless you have heard thunder
roll down from the hills
no musician can cause you to fear the angry gods.

Unless you live life raw
Art cannot compensate you for your loss.

In these empty days the mind is set free.
It fills the time with imaginings

Sloughs

One foot into the quicksand of the mind
and I am lost,
sinking deeper into panic and confusion.
The sucking waters, cunning, shifting,
pull me from below.

'Don't struggle or you'll drown the faster.'

Still time for rescue.
I've seen it in the movies.
Someone with a plank will come,
crawl across to me,
put a harness round me
winch me from the jealous pot.
Save me from myself,
from the underworld of guilt
the grey caverns of memory,
where in my mind
lives the minotaur.

Calm Waters

Today the sea is a sheet of aluminium foil
unfolding without fuss onto the beach.
Yesterday a small boat struggled
through peeks and troughs
to pull in lobster creels.

Yesterday my mind careened bruisingly
and none of my creels reached home.
Today it is reflective grey
placidly unrolling, without fuss,
sliding thoughts gently into rockpools.

Moody days

Some days I swim
in the pool of my own tears,
cry, like Alice, when my grief
is grown huge.

Some days I wake high on the swing
till one word brings me down,
till I become a submariner
staring at sightless fish.

There's no light at a thousand fathoms.

Damaged synapses

Fragments of my day
unite, make memory, make history,
make myth.
Create a universe
in which I am a visitor.

In sleep this bruised and anxious mind
agitates, streams
through corridors of hopes and hatreds,
pathways of remembered wrongs,
despair, spoiled sunsets,
sweat-soaked nights,
 until the inevitable burst
disperses thought like dandelion seeds
to toss directionless to land
and propagate.

Brittle bones
hold what is me and what
is far beyond me.

Unbalanced.

Today I am unbalanced
and the world resonates,
providing disharmonies,
atonal interludes.
Potholes jar my body,
the café table rocks,
the plate they bring my food on
is too small, a chip slides off.
The floor is grimy.
Being helpful I pick up the chip
lay it by my plate.
My stomach turns at the blackened thing.

My cage is rattled.
I'm not patient with preciousness,
the sentimental, or the 'poor me.'
Not tolerant of those who need
to mythologise their lives.
Today it's good to be obliged
to keep myself apart
from polite company.

Mirages.

A banshee wind
curls up the masts.
Turns rigging
into prayer wheels.
Temple bells.

From plastic bags,
two crows take form.
Light through wine runs
a rainbow across my page.
Sun shatters against rocky water
a galaxy of stars.

The Road.

White lines and cat's eyes,
pull me forward
through the double-dark
of this tree-lined arterial,
through the grey wasteland of fields
flat to the silver shred of city lights
defining the horizon.
I am my own companion
reflected many times in the blackness
beyond the glass.
Outside, Grotesques that fly by night,
the one-eyed ghouls,
the shredded skin of nightmares,
fail to catch me.
I pass shrines where other travellers died,
their spirits throng against this fragile bubble
of living warmth.

River.

A river brutalises rocks,
fells trees, sculpts itself a landscape,
curling, not gently, under sandstone
making ox-bow lakes for fun,
as if a single being
etches out the pathways of Earth's brain,
forcing through connective tissues
obliging electrical impulses,
across nerve-endings, to collide.

A wilful being.
Yet where I sit
never the same water passes me twice.

Portal.

Gates on a bare hillside between fallen fences.
A willow archway leads from here to there,
from somewhere to no-where.
Today my mind is prosaic,
too mundane to see beyond
the somewhere
to what might be,
so I don't walk through them.

Light slides away
And with it slip rapacious hours
Swallowing lives.

I inhabit the wind.

Pulsing blood
visible against the sand
on which I manifest.
Rocks born of fire
milled fine,
each grain a universe
for nuclei within,
shift and sigh
become my feet.
Tides, pulled by far moons,
breathe inner seas,
waters lie weightless.
Become
my formless form.

Time lies drowned

Where bells ring silently
fish swim through halls
nibbling at tangled weed
woven around chandeliers.
Crabs hide under broken ormulu
gawp gumless mouths in mirrors
as the silver cracks.

Where time lies drowned
fish swim through hours,
under stilled minute hands.
Where muted bells wait for the rising tide
there memories remain
silted over until storms come.

I Stare out to Sea.

The sky bends round us
enfolding, comforting.
Along the shoreline
safe from sudden cliffs,
the ominous dark depths,
we rest in a promise of eternity.
Out there in the flickering sunlight
where air becomes liquid
there is no solace.

At home I long to pull down the walls
to live in that vastness.
Homeliness is alien in this moment
and I am full of melancholy
longing for the play of light
across the restless sea,
This closed-off world stifles me.

The Eye of the Storm

I want to be the storm,
get lost in it,
collide with surprised cows and parts of motor cars,
land somewhere that isn't Kansas.

I want to lose myself in paradoxical events
where frozen elements of life reveal
their turbulence
and dervishes their hollow core
of stillness.

Hurtling droplets in a waterfall
split and stretch,
melt in foam and steam.
Suspended by the artist's brush
inside the paint, the canvas and dead badger hair,
molecules and atoms whirl,
tapping a tight dance.
Their lonely nuclei navigate an empty cosmos,
never for one millisecond still.

Wormhole

Driven like cattle we plod and crawl
in sad searching
for wider, deeper, vaster territories.
For greater freedom
For understanding.

Above all I long to understand.

The last room had lots of people.
Lots of noise. Lots of glitter.
I liked it there.
Only the grit on the floor irritated me.
Got in my eyes.
The grit in the oyster
Exhorted me to leave.

How well I know this place
mud-slippery with tears.
The tunnel between dreams.
Always new. Always the same.
Love and promise of oceanic healing,
Again my atoms dance
in the temples of their own devising.

No skin or bone or sinew.
No touch, nor sight, nor sound.
This vault of silence
where breath stops

The place of form unformed
freed from the camera of our eyes,
those willing henchmen of time and space
who freeze the images and translate
so crudely that our crude young mind
is flattered,
thinking it has a hold on things,
that it can understand
the dance of death.

Night Walks along the Coastline.

Moonwashed beaches
benign shadows
the silent rush of waves,
breaking in sighs
to kiss the stony shore.
Flecks of white
like fairy flocks
spray into the night,
Brightening pebbles
where they fall.
Each fractional moment
every fragile wave
passes like a breath
into Forever.

No **Sanctuary**

Who hung the first door?
Who pulled branches across the mouth of the cave
to hide, to shield, to shut out day?
Who first preferred to watch the shadow-play
behind the fire, to abjure
the summer's rain and love by moonlight,
preferring tales of monsters knights could kill,
maidens who could be rescued,
gods that rained down fire on hubris.
Who first denied the sap that rose in spring?
Who taught his neighbour to knock?

Oak and iron gave way
to steel-framed glass and reinforced plastic.
Hollow frames covered by sustainable forest planks,
easily defeated by a kick,
mark the place
where a drawbridge once hung
across a moat, a place of hungry carp and throttling weed.

Peeling paint and worn varnish protect us now,
fortified by the custom that demands we knock.
We build our shelters,
never strong enough against the frost.
Wind and fallen leaves get through
The bullying river rises, finding us.

Time and Again

Time's gnomon we,
unable to measure the night hours,
pretend control, were early ensnared
by this something that is nothing,
that slips through our fingers,
grating skin to bone faster than sand.

Ancients watched the passage of the stars,
divining by the pathways of the spheres.
Saw Sirius, rising yearly with the sun,
presage the inundation of the Nile,
bringing dead land to life.
In these darker northern isles we,
more prosaically,
built stone calendars,
marked hours on candles,
charted the length of shadows.

Some,
dismissed this tangible intangible
as the work of the Almighty, leaving it at that,
sold it as a commodity,
carrying the Mean hours to those
who lived by its strange inevitability.
Lawyers and prostitutes,
marked, for their convenience,
time passing.
Costed its flow with clepsydras
confounding procrastinators,
the rumoured thieves of Time.

Magician, scientist, philosopher and poet
congregate from Past and Present
to deny this invisible dimension,
suggest a warp and weft of strands
tangled in one timeless instant,
leaving us to flail and stare,
bewildered,
at no-time's implacable,
linear,
advance.

Pylons

In singing mists we walked,
tasting each fizzing droplet on our tongues.
Insidious force.
Crass intruder dancing on the wires,
flying through flesh, through sinew, and through bone,
leaving neurons spinning in its slip-stream
tossing atoms in its spume,
setting inner oceans churning,
fragile vessels broken,
fractured spars
shuddering in its wake.

Circle of Life.

I bent the slender willow branch into a circle
bound it tight,
criss-crossed it with bright threads,
wove in crystals, feathers, moss,
hung it in my window to catch the moon.

Time passed, the crystals ceased to shine,
moss crumbled and the feathers died.
Too long away from air
dreams withered.

I let them go,
released the willow bough
Wanting it to spring back.
Too late.
Fused into me it had become
my circle of life.

Waiting

I've been waiting all my life, it seems
in empty, aching, god-forsaken places,
howling, crying, echoing from my dreams.
I've been waiting all my life it seems
in the shadows of those dreadful spaces.

I've been waiting all my life, it seems,
for some one, some thing, some inner rising.
I've been waiting all my life it seems,
for comets, shooting stars and men from Mars
to fill the emptiness that is my heart.

I've been waiting all my life it seems
for intensity of light,
for heights extreme.
I've been waiting all my life, it seems
to fill the inner emptiness with sight.

Words

'Language is essentially the shorthand for the higher thought processes.' Terman and Merrill 1937

Shadows
on the wall
in the cave of inspiration.

Symbols, organising strategies,
structuring ideas,
giving form,
naming, quantifying,
defining, confining,
fixing, controlling.
Limiting.

Too heavy to be grafted
onto delicate tendrils,
waved through deep waters
brain to brain,
mind to mind,
words coax the ineffable
from its inception.

Loaded with clumsy synonyms
fronds wither, stiffen, break
upon the mysteries they
quiver to communicate,
making them commonplace,
shattering frail fancies.

Shadows on the wall
in the cave of inspiration.

Locks Unpicked by Words in Hope.

A prisoner freed
from this cell of bone
Spins a universe from Hope.

The last leaf in the box
Lies quiet
As the ills of the Earth
Fly mindless into dark matter

And vanish.
Past, present, and future
Cross-currents indistinguishable
In a fevered ocean of imaginings.

Remembering Kipling's Just So story: 'How The Whale Got His Throat.'

Flotsam

Salvos.
Staccato bursts of thought,
fired from brain to tongue,
shoot into the world in symbols,
a diluted draft of emotion.

Where is the shipwrecked mariner
when you need him
to fashion a filter from a box,
let the Leviathan survive
without emptying the ocean of words?

Without emptying it of meaning.

Her seas are overfished.
Small fry and plankton all that remain.
Metaphor, simile, hyperbole, toss
lifeless on a sea of speeches.
Freed from the shipwrecked galleon of the mind,
their jagged spars wound the firmament.

The De-Sanctification of the Modern Church

In the cinnamon dawn of gaudy day
fumble-fingered doctors
play with souls.
Blatant hills
flaunt ice-cream peaks
above drab fields
turned grey by the harrow.

I quit the poem
slamming the door on that meretricious dawn
leaving doctors playing blamelessly,
hills undiminished by childish fancies.
Taking with me the imagery,
I left it bland. Sighed with relief.

I had been warned.
A policeman at the door:
'Your car was stolen in the night.
We're sorry to have to tell you madam,
(you may need to sit)
it was stolen by a Poet.
When recovered it was littered with adjectives,
the trunk full of adverbs.

Our forensic team went over it,
removed the worst of the offensive material,
took it to the lab for further investigation,
after which it will be carefully destroyed
by fire, the earth salted where the ashes fall.

The clean-up team followed them and did their best,
but we recommend you contact your insurance company.
It is our unpleasant duty to have to tell you
you may never be completely free
 of hyperbole whilst driving again.

Speaking in Tongues. 1

When I talk
people look puzzled,
as though I speak in tongues.
Each word I utter
is carefully chosen for its illuminating properties,
its wisdom and its wit.
Still no-one follows me.
So I travel alone.
Silent, as if words had never been.

Speaking in Tongues 2

Last night I looked into his eyes
holding him in my own.
Neither of us looked away.
We down-loaded essential information,
wordlessly.

White Noise.

Does it ever stop
this snail trail of reproachfulness
belief in things undone
towels not clean enough
brass unshone?
This stream of anxious self-reproach,
eroding undertow,
clamour of discordant bells.
This static.

*Every stimulus must reach a certain intensity before any appreciable sensation results. This point is known as the threshold or **liminal** intensity.* James Sully. Outlines of psychology. 1888

Liminal

Neon smiles squawking primary colours
Networking American dentistry
Marketing the image
Putting it out there
In sound bites.

To Hell with subtlety
Subliminal messaging unnecessary now.
It's all liminal
This business of selling souls.

Join the shouting or fade.
Voluntary euthanasia by Silence.

Warning Bells

Metal scratching over metal.
Chalk across a slate.
Noise of a world in chaos.
The clamour of warning bells.
Find me a mantra
to dull the pain of it.
Find me poetry and story.
Find me music.
Compose for me a cello piece,
a dark, low mellow piece.
Take me to a café
loud with gossip
where women squawk with laughter
like hyenas at a kill.
Drown out searing discord
Noise of a world in chaos.
The clamour of warning bells.

S.O.S. A Sparrow Falls.

Warm thoughts are necessary
to wrap a dressing over exposed nerves
protect them from the stinging air.
They are the opiates that bring sleep,
make waking possible.
It grows harder to conjure them,
easier to despair.

A million children starve
daily bombs amputate limbs,
decapitate, kill dreams,
destroy all peace
and rip through hope.

For Heaven's sake
cast spotlights on beauty,

on cathedrals, on churches,
make stained glass glow.
Not all we have created is ugly.
Illuminate ancient city walls
moss-covered, softened,
no longer borders.

Shine light on statues of other gods
who promised nothing
were equally cruel
yet somehow more humane
understanding as they did
the human condition, living it.

Make ruined abbeys beautiful,
halo them in luminescence,
let penumbral shadow
soothe the sight
of cardboard city sleepers
drugged against the night.

Let light
put aching hearts to rest
for a while
to Save Our Souls.

Invitation to Amuse.

In a mirage, in a dust storm, let rise
the *jinn* in smokeless, scorching fire.
Lift me from this lukewarm life
where Boredom and Listlessness
sit in state, amongst the bleached bones
of fallen gods.

Please come and entertain me
with wild thoughts and sights
as yet unseen.
Make my nights merry
and my mornings glad
with will-o'-the-wisp and phantom,
dwarves and giants.

Send me stories
as yet unwritten.
Raise chimeras from
the wilderness, free of Reason.

If I answer rightly
all questions from the Sphinx
admit me please to Middle Earth,
To Narnia, and beyond.
To the undiscovered countries from whose bourn
I shall never, willingly, return.

It's not quite the end…

Printed in Poland
by Amazon Fulfillment
Poland Sp. z o.o., Wrocław

59525520R00035